P9-DWO-451

32
Super Salads

BARRON'S
Woodbury, New York • Toronto • London • Sydney

Credits
Photography
Color photographs: Irwin Horowitz
Food preparation: Andrea Swenson
Stylist: Hal Walter

Cover and book design   Milton Glaser, Inc.

Series editor   Carole Berglie

Recipe credits
Alston, Elizabeth. *The Best of Natural Eating Around the World.* © 1973 by Elizabeth Alston. Reprinted by permission of the David McKay Company, Inc. (p. 63)

Araldo, Josephine. *Cooking with Josephine.* © 1977 by Josephine Araldo. Reprinted by permission of Strawberry Hill Press. (p. 49)

Chen, Pearl, T.C. Chen, and Rose Tseng. *The Cuisine of China.* © 1983 by Barron's Educational Series, Inc. Reprinted by permission. (p. 45)

Claiborne, Craig. *The New York Times Cook Book.* © 1961 by Craig Claiborne. Published by Harper & Row, Publishers. Reprinted by permission. (p. 39)

Claiborne, Craig. *The New York Times International Cook Book.* © 1971 by the New York Times Company. Reprinted by permission. (p. 15)

Davidson, Alan. *Mediterranean Seafood.* © 1972 by Alan Davidson. Published by Penguin Books Ltd., London. By permission of Penguin Books Ltd. (p. 53)

Délu, Christian. *French Provincial Cuisine.* © 1977 by Editions Denoel, Paris. U.S. edition published by Barron's Educational Series, Inc. Reprinted by permission. (pp. 37, 41)

Evans, Michele. *The Salad Book.* © 1975 by Michele Evans. Reprinted with the permission of Contemporary Books, Inc. (p. 59)

Fuhrmann, Elke. *Salads for All Occasions.* © Falken, West Germany. U.S. rights by Barron's Educational Series, Inc. Reprinted by permission. (pp. 7, 9, 25, 29, 43, 47, 51, 55, 61)

Giusti-Lanham, Hedy and Andrea Dodi. *The Cuisine of Venice.* © 1978 by Barron's Educational Series, Inc. Reprinted with permission. (p. 11)

Giusti-Lanham, Hedy. *Cooking for Company.* © 1983 by Barron's Educational Series, Inc. Reprinted with permission. (p. 19)

Hazelton, Nika. *The Regional Italian Kitchen.* © 1978 by Nika Standen Hazelton. Published by M. Evans and Company, Inc. Reprinted with permission. (p. 17)

Kennedy, Diana. *The Cuisines of Mexico.* © 1972 by Diana Kennedy. Published by Harper & Row, Publishers, Inc. Reprinted by permission of Harper & Row, Publishers. (p. 31)

Meyers, Perla. *The Peasant Kitchen.* © 1975 by Perla Meyers. Reprinted by permission of Harper & Row, Publishers, Inc. (pp. 21, 35)

Olney, Judith. *Judith Olney's Entertainments.* © 1981 by Barron's Educational Series, Inc. Reprinted with permission. (p. 27)

Reekie, Jennie. *Everything Raw: The No-Cooking Cookbook.* © 1977 by Jennie Reekie. Reprinted by permission of Penguin Books. (p. 63)

Romagnoli, Margaret and G. Franco. *The Romagnolis' Table.* © 1974 by Margaret and G. Franco Romagnoli. Reprinted by permission of Atlantic Monthly Press. (p. 13)

St. Paul's Greek Orthodox Church, The Recipe Club of. *The Regional Cuisines of Greece.* © 1981 by The Recipe Club. Published by Doubleday & Company, Inc. Reprinted by permission. (p. 23)

Swedlin, Rosalie. *A World of Salads.* © 1980 by Rosalie Swedlin. Published by Holt, Rinehart and Winston. Reprinted by permission. (p. 33)

© Copyright 1983 by Barron's Educational Series, Inc.

All rights reserved.
No part of this book may be reproduced in any form, by photostat, microfilm, xerography, or any other means, or incorporated into any information retrieval system, electronic or mechanical, without the written permission of the copyright owner.

All inquiries should be addressed to:

Barron's Educational Series, Inc.
113 Crossways Park Drive
Woodbury, New York 11797

International Standard Book No. 0-8120-5529-2

Library of Congress Catalog Card No. 83-2535

Library of Congress Cataloging in Publication Data
Main entry under title:

32 super salads.

(Barron's cooking the easy way series)
1. Salads. I. Title: Thirty-two super salads.
II. Series.
TX740.A15   1983   641.8'3   83-2535
ISBN 0-8120-5529-2

PRINTED IN THE
UNITED STATES OF AMERICA
3 4 5 6   RAE   9 8 7 6 5 4 3 2 1

INTRODUCTION

Feel like having a salad for dinner tonight? Make it your main course, or an appetizer, or the palate-refresher between dinner and dessert. Salads aren't new to the foods of the world, but our uses of them have broadened so much that about the only role they don't play is at breakfast.

A salad can be as simple as a colorful bowl of tossed greens or as complex as a main dish that takes hours to prepare. They are the predictable picnic cole slaw and potato salad or an unusual Korean meat salad with slivers of top sirloin, Chinese mushrooms, capers, shallots, and sesame oil (page 15). Salads can be a big bowl of curly chicory leaves pungent with garlic and accompanied by anchovy-filled pastries (page 41), or a shimmering vegetable sculpture molded of peas, carrots, green beans, potatoes, and herbs (page 49).

Serve your salads as they suit you. In countries such as Italy and France they have usually been presented after the main course—as a refreshment for the diner's eyes and taste buds. In the United States, however, salads are often served before the main course. But you may want your salad alongside the main dish—as a leafy contrast to fish or pasta, for instance. Salads also work well as light luncheons, satisfying the big appetites but light enough not to be a drag on the rest of your afternoon. The Eggplant and Shellfish Salad (page 21) is a zesty meal in whatever form you serve it: in small portions as an appetizer, in moderate quantities as a lunch, or as a one-dish dinner accompanied by gutsy French bread.

Salads are a symphony of tastes and textures, where individual flavors are recognized but the combined effect is pleasant harmony. With such contrasting but complementary flavors as fennel, smoked ham, and fresh oranges, you have a salad that is at once crunchy, fragrant, hearty, and light (page 47). The Italian Rice Salad brings together pickled vegetables and rice, tuna, and eggs, binding them melodiously with a dressing of lemon juice and olive oil (page 13).

Salads can be a dieter's salvation, since they provide endless variations on a single basic theme. There's lots of eating without loads of calories. Even with an oil-based dressing, salads are often very low in calories and yet packed with nutrition. Flaked with smoked fish or tossed with slivers of ham, salads will allow dieters to sample their favorite tastes without spending a whole day's calorie allotment on one meal. The Celery and Apple Mix-Up (page 37) and Vegetable Salad in Aspic (page 49) are two such recipes with low calorie counts, but you can alter a number of the recipes in this book to match your own needs. Substitute a low-calorie dressing or simply cut back on the dressing to suit your tastes.

It is easy to make ordinary salads—but haven't you already ventured past that point? Make yourself and your family some *super* salads, with fresh ingredients that are readily available in your local market, and clear instructions that are easy to follow. The recipes in this book represent a congenial blending of the classic and the contemporary, the familiar and the novel. You'll sample the preferences of the Mediterranean, the influences of the Orient, and the favorites of the Americas. You'll use meats, cheese, fish, grains, fruits, and vegetables in new contexts, and try out different greens with familiar herbs and spices. Salads are custom-made for adventure; you just can't go wrong.

C.B.

SALAD MAKINGS

For most salads, the greens are at least a starting point, if not the main component. You'll want to buy firm greens that are bright in color, with no dark or wilted edges. The heads should be tight, the leaves firmly adhering in a cluster. The bases, where the lettuce would have been severed from its roots, should be a fresh cut, not browned over days of storage. When you bring your greens home, don't wash them unless you plan to use them that evening. If the greens are wet, allow them to dry first; then wrap them in a paper towel and put either in the crisper drawer or in a plastic bag in your refrigerator. The paper towel will absorb any extra moisture, keeping the greens crisp through storage. Then when you are ready to prepare your salad, wash the greens under cool running water or submerge them in a basin of water to allow the dirt to lift off. Place the leaves on paper toweling to dry completely. After you have made your salad, in most cases you'll want to chill the lettuce briefly in the refrigerator before serving.

You'll want to vary your choice of greens, so we've given you a brief run-down on those you're most likely to find in your market:

Arugula/Rocket   An Italian favorite but appearing increasingly in all markets. It has a slim notched leaf with a peppery flavor.

Belgian Endive   With a very delicate taste, this usually expensive green has the appearance of an icicle because it is the second year's growth of the chicory plant, sprouted in the absence of light.

Butterhead Lettuces   These include Boston and Bibb, two light-flavored favorites for all-around use. The heads are loose and the leaves accumulate soil as they grow, so wash them carefully before using.

Chicory   Also called curly-leaved endive, this is usually added to a salad as an accent, since the leaves have a pungent flavor. Also good solo, with a garlic accent (see page 41).

Escarole   Also called broad-leaved endive, this is like chicory in that it is a form of endive. It also has a sharp, bitter taste and is best as a subtle highlight.

Iceberg Lettuce   Unpopular at present as a salad green, this very mild lettuce is exceedingly crisp and the leaves have a high water content, making it very refreshing for summer. Good in contrast with other greens or with a creamy dressing.

Looseleaf Lettuces   These are now in the markets, and used widely. Most common varieties of this lettuce, which does not form a head, are the ruby and salad bowl lettuces. The leaves are frilly, often tinted with red.

Oakleaf Lettuce   This is also a looseleaf lettuce, not too common in markets. The leaves resemble an oak leaf, but their color is bright green and their taste has a pleasant sharpness.

Romaine   A good all-purpose lettuce with a characteristic flavor that does not predominate a salad. The crisp long leaves are best taken from the interior; the outer ones are often too bitter or coarse.

Sorrel   Also called sour grass, this is the basis for soups as well. Its flavor is somewhat lemony and mildly acidic, so it adds a surprising contrast with other lettuces. The arrow-shaped leaves are best when small, stems removed.

Watercress   With dark green leaves and a pepper taste, this green is usually expensive but well worth the cost because it adds such color and textural contrast. Very perishable.

WILD GREENS

There are many greens coming back into usage, and some can be collected right in your neighborhood. Among the resident delicacies are dandelion leaves (pick the young ones in the spring) and purslane, a fleshy ground-spreading weed with a pleasantly sharp flavor and lots of vitamin C. Check the wild foods cookbooks, and wash greens carefully.

HERBS

Parsley and dill are usually in markets all year round, but when they are in season, watch for basil, borage, chives, coriander, marjoram, mint, oregano, rosemary, savory, tarragon, and thyme. Chop the leaves and add them to the salad or dressing.

FLOWERS

Especially if you have your own flower garden, you can have fun adding small floral touches to your salads. Not every flower is edible (check in cookbooks first), but you should occasionally try nasturtium flowers for their orangey red accent or violets (see page 27) for a dramatic effect, or marigold petals for their autumnal images. Daylilies are a surprise; they taste like mildly sweet chestnuts. Chrysanthemums and rose petals also are used frequently.

ACCENTS

There are foods that can instantly give your salad a savory focus without dominating it. Some of these accents are olives, anchovies, bacon bits, capers, pickle slices, or tuna. Other accents are visual and textural: croutons, sesame seeds, sunflower hearts, nuts.

DRESSINGS

Almost all salad dressings are composed of two basic elements: vinegar and oil. The best-known dressing is a simple vinaigrette—a blending of oil, vinegar, salt, pepper and sometimes mustard or garlic or herbs or an egg. Mayonnaise too is a fundamental emulsion of egg yolks, spiked with vinegar and whisked with oil until fluffy. There are dressings made from cream, yogurt, and other such ingredients, but these are usually ideally paired with certain salads and accompany the recipes in the book.

Vinegars   Most vinegar is made by fermenting either red or white wine. Generally the red wine vinegars are stouter in flavor, and when you have a salad of delicate greens it is best to use a white wine vinegar. Sometimes these vinegars are infused with other flavorings, such as from raspberries or herbs like basil or thyme. Lastly there are also vinegars made from rice, which come to us from the East, and these are milder and more limited in use. Often, to soften the acidic side of your dressing, you may substitute lemon or lime juice for vinegar.

Oils   Olive oil is the type used frequently in salad dressings, since its flavor is assertive but pleasant. Those labeled "first pressing" are the best for salads; they are golden in color and light in taste. Many people, however, prefer to use other kinds of oil, such as safflower, sunflower, peanut, corn, or walnut oil, which are all lower in cholesterol than olive oil (safflower is the lowest). Except for peanut oil, these are much milder in flavor and are best used when blended into a mayonnaise or in a dressing where other flavors will predominate. Walnut oil is a relatively new oil to be found in neighborhood markets. It is more perishable, but good when its nutty character is allowed to come through.

YIELD
4 servings

PREPARATION
15 minutes

INGREDIENTS
4 heads Bibb lettuce
1 bunch watercress
2 hard-cooked egg yolks

DRESSING
¼ cup olive oil
¼ teaspoon salt
¼ teaspoon white pepper

Trim the lettuce heads and cut each in half. Wash and drain well ①.

Trim the watercress ②, removing lower portions of the stems. Wash and drain.

Place the lettuce halves on a platter and tuck the watercress around them. Push the egg yolks through a small strainer ③ or crumble over the lettuce. Chill.

Mix the olive oil with the salt and pepper. Sprinkle over the lettuce before serving.

YIELD
4 servings

PREPARATION
10 minutes

MARINATING
1 hour

INGREDIENTS
1½ pounds cooked potatoes
Salt
2 cups fresh or frozen peas
2 bunches radishes
2 tablespoons chopped watercress
2 tablespoons chopped fresh parsley

DRESSING
⅓ cup white wine
2 tablespoons white wine vinegar
½ cup oil
¼ teaspoon pepper

Peel and slice the potatoes ①. Sprinkle slices with salt.

Mix dressing and pour over potatoes ②. Let marinate 1 hour, stirring potatoes from time to time.

Blanch the peas in boiling water. Rinse with cold water to keep color green ③, then drain and mix with potatoes.

Slice the radishes and add to the potatoes. Add half the watercress and parsley, then mix with salad and chill. Just before serving, season again and garnish with additional parsley and watercress.

YIELD
4 servings

PREPARATION
10 minutes

COOKING
20 minutes

INGREDIENTS
4 fresh zucchini, not longer than 4 to
   5 inches
4 large carrots, peeled
1 cup sliced young fresh green beans
½ pound fresh, young spinach leaves,
   washed and drained
Salt and freshly ground black pepper
2 tablespoons wine vinegar
½ cup olive oil

Wash the zucchini and scrape off any rough spots but don't peel. Bring water to a boil and add the whole zucchini. Boil for 5 to 6 minutes, according to size. If you can stick a fork in easily, they are done. Remove, let cool, and slice into pieces ⅓ inch thick.

Slice the carrots into pieces about the size of the zucchini, then cook in boiling water for 5 to 6 minutes until tender. Drain and let cool.

Cook the green beans in boiling water until tender, about 6 to 8 minutes. Drain and let cool.

Place the cooked vegetables in a salad bowl and add the spinach leaves. Stir to mix completely.

Place the desired amount of salt and pepper into a serving spoon. Fill the spoon with the vinegar, and with a fork stir to dissolve ① the salt in the spoon. Pour this over the salad.

Holding a cruet of oil a few inches above the bowl, pour a thin stream of olive oil over the salad ②. Taste and, if you want more sharpness, add more vinegar ③. The taste of these fresh young vegetables is so delicate that a little vinegar will go a long way. Mix very well and serve.

From *The Cuisine of Venice* by Hedy Giusti-Lanham and Andrea Dodi

YIELD
6 to 8 servings

PREPARATION
10 minutes

COOKING
30 minutes

INGREDIENTS

2 cups long-grain rice
2 hard-cooked eggs
2 anchovy fillets
½ cup mixed black and green olives
1 cup Italian pickled vegetables
2 tablespoons capers
½ green sweet pepper
½ red sweet pepper
1 package (10 ounces) frozen mixed
    vegetables (2 cups)

1 can (7 ounces) dark Italian tuna
½ cup olive oil
Juice of 2 lemons
Salt and freshly ground pepper

Cook the rice in at least 6 cups of salted water, and drain in a colander the minute it's done ①, rinsing the cooked rice with cold water to wash off any remaining liquid and to separate the grains. Drain thoroughly and put in a big salad bowl.

Chop the hard-cooked eggs ② and anchovies, and add them to the rice. Cut the olives in half, and add along with the pickles and capers. Slice the peppers into thin strips, and add.

Cook the frozen mixed vegetables until tender, but be careful not to overcook them. Drain and add to the rice mixture.

Drain the tuna fish and break it up with a fork before adding to the bowl ③. Pour in the olive oil, enough to dress the salad well. Add the lemon juice, taste for seasonings, and adjust if necessary before tossing again. Chill for at least 30 minutes, and serve.

From *The Romagnolis' Table* by Margaret and G. Franco Romagnoli

KOREAN MEAT SALAD

5

YIELD
8 to 10 servings

PREPARATION
15 minutes

SOAKING
15 minutes

COOKING
10 minutes

MARINATING
1 day

INGREDIENTS

3 pounds top sirloin, eye round of beef, or other lean, good-quality beef
2 tablespoons peanut oil
5 dried mushrooms, preferably Chinese
4 jars (4½ ounces) sliced mushrooms
3 tablespoons soy sauce
1 tablespoon rice or white vinegar
1 tablespoon vinegar from bottled capers
3 cloves garlic, crushed

2 red onions, finely chopped
1 yellow onion, sliced into rings
6 green onions, green and white parts, trimmed and sliced
1 tablespoon finely chopped shallots
2 tablespoons finely chopped parsley
3 tablespoons capers
2 teaspoons sesame oil

Trim the meat of all fat, then cut the meat into very thin strips, approximately ¼ by ¼ by 2 inches ①. Heat the oil in a skillet and cook the beef, stirring just until it loses color ②. Transfer the meat to a mixing bowl.

Place the dried mushrooms in another mixing bowl and add lukewarm water to cover. Let stand 15 minutes or longer. Remove the mushrooms; discard their stems and slice the caps. Reserve.

To the skillet in which the meat cooked add the liquid from the jar of mushrooms. Add the soy sauce, vinegars, and juices that may have accumulated around the beef. Do not add the beef. Bring this liquid to a boil.

Combine the garlic, onions, green onions, shallots, parsley, capers, dried mushrooms, and mushrooms from the jar. Pour the skillet liquid over them ③ and let stand until cool. Add the mixture to the beef, then stir in the sesame oil. Cover and refrigerate at least 24 hours, but serve at room temperature.

From *New York Times International Cook Book* by Craig Claiborne

YIELD
4 servings

PREPARATION
5 minutes

COOKING
5 minutes

INGREDIENTS
2½ pounds broccoli
½ to ⅔ cup olive oil
3 to 4 tablespoons strained fresh
    lemon juice
Salt and freshly ground pepper

Remove the outer leaves from the broccoli ①, then cut the florets apart and split the larger stems lengthwise ②. Cut the pieces into 3-inch lengths ③ so all pieces are about a uniform size.

Cook the broccoli in just enough boiling salted water to cover for 4 to 5 minutes, or until tender but still crisp. Drain, and put the broccoli into a serving dish.

Combine the oil, lemon juice, and a little salt and pepper, and pour over the broccoli. Serve hot or cold.

From *The Regional Italian Kitchen* by Nika Hazelton

YIELD

4 servings

PREPARATION

5 minutes

COOKING

10 minutes

INGREDIENTS

2 cups broth or water
1 cup buckwheat
1 small cucumber
½ cup minced parsley
1 tablespoon wine vinegar
⅓ cup olive oil

Bring the broth or water to a boil in a saucepan. Add the buckwheat ① and cook over high heat until it is *al dente,* meaning firm. This should take about 10 minutes; don't overcook.

Drain well and spread the buckwheat out to cool completely ②.

Peel and seed the cucumber ③, then chop very fine. If you have a food processor, cut the cucumber into 3 or 4 pieces and, using the sharp blade, turn the motor on and off a couple of times until the cucumber is chopped fine but not puréed. (The parsley may also be minced very fine in the food processor.)

Place the buckwheat in a salad bowl and add the cucumber and parsley. Sprinkle in the vinegar and toss. Add the olive oil, toss, and taste. Your palate might demand a little more vinegar; add as needed.

Let the salad stand awhile, but toss again just before serving.

From *Cooking for Company* by Hedy Giusti-Lanham

YIELD
8 servings

PREPARATION
15 minutes

DRAINING
2 hours

COOKING
40 minutes

CHILLING
8 hours

INGREDIENTS

3 medium eggplants, peeled and cut
    into 1-inch cubes
Salt
1 cup olive oil, approximately
½ cup thinly sliced almonds
2 cups sliced onions
2 cloves garlic, finely minced
2 cups finely diced celery
2 medium tomatoes, peeled, seeded,
    and chopped
⅔ cup tomato purée
2 tablespoons well-drained capers

1 cup small black olives (oil-cured)
2 large red peppers, charred, seeded,
    and sliced
Freshly ground black pepper
1 small can (3½ ounces) tuna
1 cup cooked, peeled, diced shrimp

GARNISH
Juice of ½ lemon
Finely minced fresh parsley
Finely sliced rounds of red pepper
Rolled anchovy fillets

Place the eggplant on a double layer of paper towels, sprinkle with salt, and let drain for 1 or 2 hours ①.

While eggplant is draining, heat 2 tablespoons of the oil in a small heavy skillet. Add the almonds and cook them until lightly browned ②, then remove them to a double layer of paper towels to drain.

Dry the eggplant thoroughly with paper towels. In a large heavy skillet, heat ¼ cup of the oil. Add the eggplant cubes, a few at a time (do not crowd your pan), and sauté until they are nicely browned ③. Remove to a colander and continue sautéing, adding a little more oil when necessary.

When all the eggplant is done, add a little more oil to the pan, then the onion and cook over low heat until soft and lightly browned. Add the garlic, celery, tomatoes, and tomato purée; cover the skillet and cook the mixture until the celery is tender, about 10 minutes.

Return the eggplant to the pan, together with the capers, olives, and red peppers. Season with salt and pepper and simmer the mixture for another 5 minutes, then add the almonds, tuna, shrimp. Heat through, correct the seasonings, and pour into a bowl. Chill for 6 to 8 hours.

Just before serving toss the salad lightly, sprinkle with either lemon juice and parsley, or garnish with thinly sliced red pepper rounds and rolled anchovy fillets.

From *The Peasant Kitchen* by Perla Meyers

YIELD

8 servings

PREPARATION

10 minutes

INGREDIENTS

2 pounds fresh spinach
1/2 cup olive oil
2 tablespoons white wine vinegar
2 tablespoons lemon juice
1/4 teaspoon ground cinnamon
1/4 teaspoon powdered mustard
Salt and pepper
2 cucumbers
4 hard-cooked eggs
1/4 pound feta cheese, crumbled
2 green onions, chopped

Remove the stems from the spinach ①. Wash and drain leaves, then cut into 1-inch-wide strips ②. Put the spinach in a salad bowl.

Blend together the oil, vinegar, lemon juice, and spices. Pour half the dressing over the spinach and mix well.

Thinly slice the cucumbers (with or without peel) and arrange on top of the spinach. Slice the eggs and arrange on top of the cucumbers ③.

Sprinkle salad with cheese and onions. Pour remaining dressing over salad.

From *The Regional Cuisines of Greece* by The Recipe Club of St. Paul's Greek Orthodox Church

SALAMI-GREEN BEAN SALAD

YIELD
4 servings

PREPARATION
10 minutes

CHILLING
1 hour

INGREDIENTS
1 can (1 pound) cut green beans
8 ounces salami in 1 piece
2 medium onions

DRESSING
6 tablespoons oil
3 tablespoons vinegar
1 clove garlic, crushed
Salt and black pepper

Drain the beans. Cut the salami into thin strips ①. Thinly slice the onions ②. Mix all ingredients in a bowl.

Beat oil and vinegar with garlic. Season to taste with salt and pepper. Toss salad with dressing ③. Chill 1 hour before serving.

YIELD
8 servings

PREPARATION
30 minutes

COOKING
25 minutes

CHILLING
1 hour

INGREDIENTS
32 walnut halves
1 ½ pounds tender green beans
2 tablespoons all-purpose flour
Juice of 1 lemon
8 artichokes
Bibb or Boston lettuce
Small goat banons or slices of Saint-
    Saviol Bucheron
Parsley and chives, chopped
Lavender-colored flower blossoms
    (violets, chives, borage, or hyssop
    blossoms)

DRESSING
⅓ cup red wine vinegar
Salt and pepper
⅓ cup olive oil
⅓ cup walnut oil
Minced herbs (parsley, chives)

Prepare a walnut-oil vinaigrette by adding salt and pepper to the vinegar and stirring until the salt dissolves. Stir in the oils and the herbs, and mix with a fork until well blended. Taste for seasoning.

Bring a small pot of water to a boil and plunge in the walnuts. Boil for 3 minutes, then drain and peel.

Cook the beans in salted boiling water until just tender. Drain and cool.

Bring a large pot of salted water to a boil. Mix the flour with ¼ cup of water and add the paste and lemon juice to the pot. Using a stainless-steel knife, cut off the artichoke stems ①, snap back the leaves, and cut off 1½ inches of each's top ②. Trim the artichokes of dark leaf portions until only the hearts remain ③. Cook in the boiling water until a knife point easily pierces the stem end. Strain from the water and lift off the choke portions.

Immediately add artichokes to the vinaigrette, turning them well in the oil; then add the beans and marinate at room temperature for at least 1 hour.

To serve, prepare a small bed of lettuce leaves on each plate. Place goat cheese portion in the middle, then swirl green beans around it. Garnish with artichokes, walnuts, herbs, and lavender flowers. Drizzle any remaining dressing over each portion.

From *Judith Olney's Entertainments*

CRUNCHY BEEF SALAD

YIELD
4 servings

PREPARATION
30 minutes

CHILLING
30 minutes

INGREDIENTS
1 small cucumber
10 ounces boiled beef
1 can (14 ounces) hearts of palm
5 tomatoes
3 onions
6 sprigs curly parsley
1 tablespoon fresh dill

DRESSING
1/4 cup vinegar
Salt and black pepper
Pinch of sugar (optional)
1 cup sour cream

Peel the cucumber ①, using a fork to scrape away the outer coating. Halve it lengthwise and scoop out the seeds with a spoon. Cut it into thin slices.

Cut the meat into thin slices, then into julienne strips.

Drain the hearts of palm and slice thinly.

Dip the tomatoes into boiling water for a few seconds ②, then strip off the skins ③. Core the tomatoes and cut into wedges.

Chop the onions finely, then combine all salad ingredients. Chop the parsley and dill and set half of each aside for a garnish.

Add the vinegar, salt, pepper, and sugar (if desired) to the salad. Toss and chill for 30 minutes.

Mix the sour cream with the remaining parsley and dill, then season to taste with salt and pepper. Pour dressing over salad and toss. Just before serving, sprinkle with the reserved parsley and dill.

STUFFED CHILI SALAD

YIELD
6 servings

PREPARATION
15 minutes

SOAKING
30 minutes

MARINATING
2 days

INGREDIENTS

6 tablespoons water
2 tablespoons vinegar, preferably wine
1 clove garlic, peeled and sliced
$1/8$ teaspoon marjoram
$1/8$ teaspoon oregano
$1/2$ bay leaf
$1/4$ teaspoon salt
3 tablespoons olive oil
6 small chilies poblanos, roasted and peeled; or canned, peeled green chilies

Lettuce leaves
Pomegranate seeds or chopped fresh coriander

STUFFING

$1/4$ onion, finely chopped
1 large avocado
$1/4$ teaspoon salt
$1/4$ teaspoon lime juice

Mix together in a glass bowl a marinade of the water, vinegar, garlic, marjoram, oregano, bay leaf, salt, and olive oil. Set aside.

Remove the seeds and veins from the chilies poblanos, if you are using them, and if they are very *picante* leave them to soak in salted water for about 30 minutes. Put the chilies into the marinade mixture and leave at least 2 days, turning from time to time. If the marinade appears to be too *picante*, replace it with fresh.

Crush the chopped onion for the stuffing and cut open the avocado ①; scoop out the flesh ②. Mash with the salt and lime juice ③.

Drain the chilies and stuff them well with the guacamole. Arrange on a bed of lettuce leaves on a serving dish and decorate with pomegranate seeds or chopped coriander.

From *The Cuisines of Mexico* by Diana Kennedy

YIELD

4 to 6 servings

PREPARATION

5 minutes

COOKING

10 minutes

INGREDIENTS

½ pound meat-filled tortellini
1 tablespoon olive oil
2 tablespoons ricotta cheese
6 to 8 tablespoons light cream
¼ pound fresh button mushrooms,
  thinly sliced
3 to 4 slices prosciutto, chopped
½ pound cooked young peas, fresh or
  frozen

1 tablespoon chopped Italian parsley
1 teaspoon dried oregano
Salt and freshly ground pepper

Use fresh tortellini if possible. Cook for several minutes in lightly salted boiling water just until tender. Drain and place in a large bowl. Add the olive oil ① and toss well.

In a separate small bowl, add the cream ② to the ricotta cheese and blend with a wooden spoon until smooth. Pour the dressing over the pasta and toss again ③.

Add the mushrooms, prosciutto, and peas. Season with parsley, oregano, salt, and plenty of freshly ground pepper. Toss thoroughly and serve.

From *A World of Salads* by Rosalie Swedlin

ZUCCHINI AND TOMATO SALAD

YIELD
6 servings

PREPARATION
5 minutes

COOKING
15 minutes

CHILLING
30 minutes

INGREDIENTS
6 small zucchini
Juice of 1 lemon
Salt and freshly ground pepper
1 small red onion, thinly sliced
Finely minced fresh parsley
½ cup finely diced pimiento
4 to 6 Italian plum tomatoes,
   quartered

DRESSING
½ cup olive oil
3 tablespoons red wine vinegar
1 large clove garlic, mashed
2 tablespoons finely minced fresh basil
   or 1 teaspoon dried

Wash the zucchini thoroughly in cold water ① and slice off both tips. Bring 4 quarts of salted water to a boil, add the zucchini, and cook over medium heat for 10 to 15 minutes, or until they are easily pierced with the tip of a sharp knife. Be careful not to overcook.

As soon as the zucchini are done, run them under cold water to stop them from further cooking. Drain and place on a double layer of paper towels to cool.

As soon as the zucchini are cool enough to handle, cut them in half lengthwise and sprinkle with lemon juice, salt, and pepper ②. Set aside.

In a small jar or cruet, combine the olive oil, vinegar, garlic, and basil ③. Shake the jar to blend and chill for 30 minutes.

Before serving, sprinkle the zucchini with the onion rings, parsley, and pimiento. Arrange the quartered tomatoes around them and pour the dressing over both vegetables. Season with salt and freshly ground black pepper. Serve chilled but not cold.

From *The Peasant Kitchen* by Perla Meyers

CELERY AND APPLE MIX-UP

YIELD
4 servings

PREPARATION
20 minutes

INGREDIENTS
1 head celery
2 tart apples
20 walnuts
7 ounces mimolette or cheddar cheese
Salt and pepper
2 tablespoons oil
1 tablespoon vinegar or lemon juice

Wash and trim the celery. Cut the celery into julienne strips ①.

Core but do not peel the apples. Dice and sprinkle lightly with lemon juice.

Shell the nuts, trying to keep them in halves or whole pieces ②.

Cut the cheese into cubes.

Make the dressing by blending together the salt, pepper, oil, and vinegar or lemon juice. Mix the apples, celery, walnuts, and cheese in a salad bowl and pour dressing over just before serving ③.

From *French Provincial Cuisine* by Christian Délu

SALMON MOUSSE WITH A SOUR-CREAM DILL SAUCE

YIELD
8 servings

PREPARATION
20 minutes

CHILLING
1 to 2 hours

INGREDIENTS

1 envelope unflavored gelatin
1/4 cup cold water
1/2 cup boiling water
1/2 cup mayonnaise
1 tablespoon lemon juice
1 tablespoon grated onion
1/2 teaspoon Tabasco sauce
1/4 teaspoon paprika
1 teaspoon salt
2 cups canned salmon, drained and
   finely chopped
1 tablespoon chopped capers

1/2 cup heavy cream
3 cups cottage cheese

SAUCE

1 egg
1 teaspoon salt
Pinch of freshly ground black pepper
Pinch of sugar
4 teaspoons lemon juice
1 teaspoon grated onion
2 tablespoons finely cut dill
1 1/2 cups sour cream

Soften the gelatin in the cold water, add the boiling water and stir until the gelatin has dissolved ①. Cool.

Mix together the mayonnaise, lemon juice, onion, Tabasco, paprika, and salt ② and add to gelatin mixture. Chill to the consistency of unbeaten egg whites.

Add the salmon and capers and beat well. Whip the cream, fold into the salmon mixture, and turn into a 2-quart oiled mold. Add the cottage cheese to fill the mold. Chill until set.

Prepare the sauce by beating the egg until fluffy and lemon-colored. Add the remaining ingredients, blending in the sour cream last. Stir until blended and chill.

Unmold the mousse onto a serving platter and garnish with watercress, lemon slices, and dill. Serve with dill sauce.

From *The New York Times Cook Book* by Craig Claiborne

YIELD
4 servings

PREPARATION
20 minutes

BAKING
25 minutes

INGREDIENTS

I cup all-purpose flour
½ cup butter or margarine
Salt and pepper
2 cloves garlic, I chopped and I
    crushed
2½ cans (2 ounces each) anchovy
    fillets, drained
3 tablespoons butter
I egg, lightly beaten
I head chicory
2 tablespoons oil
I tablespoon vinegar

Preheat the oven to 350 degrees.

Prepare the pastry first by cutting the butter into the flour ①. Add a dash of salt and the chopped garlic. Season to taste with pepper. Knead lightly to form a smooth dough, then spread it onto a buttered baking sheet, making a rectangle about 12 by 15 inches.

Blend the anchovies with the 3 tablespoons butter until it is a smooth purée. Spread the purée over the pastry ②, to within ½ inch of the edges. Fold the pastry over ③ and press together lightly. Glaze pastry with beaten egg and bake for 25 minutes in moderate oven. When lightly brown and crisp, remove from oven and let cool. Cut into squares.

Wash the chicory and drain well. Break apart and place leaves into a salad bowl.

Prepare an oil and vinegar dressing, season with salt and pepper, and add the crushed clove of garlic. Toss the salad with the dressing just before serving, and accompany with anchovy pastries.

From *French Provincial Cuisine* by Christian Délu

STUFFED TOMATOES

YIELD
4 servings

PREPARATION
15 minutes

INGREDIENTS
2 firm tomatoes
1/3 cup diced cooked chicken breast
1/4 cup heavy cream
1 tablespoon catsup
2 teaspoons chopped chives
Salt
Pinch of sweet paprika
3 stuffed green olives

Cut the tops off the tomatoes ①, and discard tops. Scoop out the flesh of the tomato and discard seeds ②; use pulp for another purpose. Lightly salt the insides of the tomatoes and turn upside down to drain briefly.

Mix the chicken, cream, catsup, and chives. Season to taste with salt and paprika, then spoon the mixture into the tomatoes ③. Serve garnished with sliced olives.

YIELD
6 servings

PREPARATION
25 minutes

COOKING
10 minutes

INGREDIENTS
1 small chicken, cooked and cooled
4 tablespoons sesame seeds
8 to 10 sprigs Chinese parsley
3 whole scallions
3 cups oil
2 ounces Chinese rice sticks
1 small head iceberg lettuce
Freshly ground black pepper

DRESSING
3 tablespoons lemon juice
1 1/2 tablespoons dry mustard
1 tablespoon water
1/4 cup peanut oil
1 tablespoon sesame oil
1 tablespoon granulated sugar
1 teaspoon chicken bouillon powder
2 tablespoons light soy sauce
1/2 teaspoon salt
1 clove garlic, minced

Skin and bone the chicken and tear the meat into julienne shreds. Reserve any juices from the chicken. Set aside.

Toast the sesame seeds in a small pan over medium heat until light brown ①, about 1 minute; do not allow to burn. Set aside.

Mix the ingredients for the dressing in a bottle and chill in refrigerator.

Clean the parsley and break the leaves from the stems. Discard the stems; you should have about 1 cup of leaves.

Trim and shred the scallions finely. Set aside.

Set a wok or deep skillet over high heat. When the wok is very hot, add the oil. Wait for about 10 minutes, then test the temperature by throwing a few inches of rice sticks into the oil. The temperature is hot enough if the rice sticks puff up immediately (about 400 degrees). Otherwise wait a little longer and test again.

When the oil is hot and smoke starts to appear on the surface, add about 1/4 of the rice sticks. They should puff up and cover the surface of the oil instantly. Turn them quickly ② and deep-fry the other side until puffy. Remove from oil quickly; you want the sticks creamy white, not brown. Finish frying the remaining rice sticks and keep all warm in a warm oven.

Shred the lettuce just before serving; you should have about 3 cups of greens. Combine the shredded lettuce and scallions, parsley leaves, shredded chicken, chicken juices, and sesame seeds in a large bowl. Add dressing and black pepper to taste and toss well. Spread rice sticks on top of salad and serve warm.

From *The Cuisine of China* by Pearl Chen, T.C. Chen, and Rose Tseng

FENNEL SALAD WITH HAM

YIELD

4 servings

PREPARATION

25 minutes

INGREDIENTS

3 knobs fennel
6 ounces smoked ham
2 navel oranges
8 stuffed green olives (optional)
5 pitted black olives (optional)

DRESSING

I clove garlic
¼ cup red wine vinegar
I teaspoon prepared mustard
½ teaspoon salt
⅛ teaspoon white pepper
⅓ cup olive oil

Trim the fennel and cut into julienne strips ①. Set aside.

Crush the garlic and mix with the vinegar, mustard, salt, pepper, and oil. Mix dressing with the fennel.

Sliver the ham ②; cut away peel and dice the oranges ③. Add ham and orange dice to the fennel. Toss and chill. Serve garnished with olives, if desired.

YIELD
8 servings

PREPARATION
20 minutes

COOKING
10 minutes

MARINATING
2 hours

CHILLING
1 hour

INGREDIENTS

2 pounds carrots, diced or sliced
1 medium potato, diced
½ pound green beans
1 pound fresh peas or 1 package
    (10 ounces) frozen
2 slices green pepper
2 cups vinaigrette dressing
1 envelope unflavored gelatin
1½ cups chicken broth or consommé
1 tablespoon chopped herbs (chives,
    parsley, and tarragon)

Cook all the vegetables separate in boiling water, adding 1 teaspoon of salt and simmering until done. Drain. Marinate vegetables in dressing for at least 2 hours.

Dissolve the gelatin in ¼ cup cold water. Bring chicken broth to a boil and then stir in the gelatin and continue to cook until completely melted. Cool the mixture until syrupy and just beginning to jell.

Pour a little of the gelatin mixture into a mold to cover the bottom ① and let it set very briefly.

Drain vegetables and place a few slices of carrot and green pepper into the mold to decorate the bottom ②. Then pour over a little more of the gelatin mixture to hold the vegetables in place. Allow to set briefly. Then spoon remaining vegetables into the mold and add remaining gelatin mixture ③. Place in refrigerator to set, about 1 hour.

To unmold, dip mold into very hot water briefly, then invert aspic onto a platter. Decorate with chopped herbs or lettuce leaves and serve with additional dressing.

From *Cooking with Josephine* by Josephine Araldo

YIELD

4 servings

PREPARATION

10 minutes

INGREDIENTS

4 hard-cooked eggs
10 pitted black olives
2 avocados
2 to 3 sprigs curly parsley
1 onion
5 or 6 lettuce or spinach leaves

DRESSING

½ cup mayonnaise
2 tablespoons lemon juice
Salt and freshly ground black pepper

Dice the eggs. Slice the olives. Scoop the pulp out of the avocados ① and dice.

Chop the parsley ② and then finely chop the onion. Mix with remaining salad ingredients but reserve the lettuce leaves.

Blend the mayonnaise with the lemon juice, adding salt and pepper to taste ③. Toss the salad with the dressing and then chill.

Line serving plates with lettuce and top with salad, or fill avocado shells with salad and serve with lettuce alongside.

TUNISIAN SALAD WITH TUNA

YIELD
4 servings

PREPARATION
20 minutes

GRILLING
10 minutes

INGREDIENTS

4 green peppers
2 tomatoes
2 cloves garlic
1 onion
Salt
1 teaspoon caraway seeds
1 can (6½ ounces) tuna, drained and
  broken into small pieces with a
  fork

2 hard-cooked eggs
Fresh lemon juice
Olive oil
Ripe olives

Over a charcoal fire or under the broiler, grill the peppers ①, tomatoes, garlic cloves, and onion for about 10 minutes, turning them occasionally. Remove the blackened skins of each ②. Halve and seed the peppers and tomatoes.

In a large mortar, pound some salt with the caraway seeds ③, then pound in the grilled garlic cloves, peppers, tomatoes, and, finally, the onion. Stir in the pieces of tuna.

Put the mixture on a platter or in a bowl and chop the hard-cooked eggs into it. Add some lemon juice and olive oil to make the whole moist, and arrange ripe olives on top.

From *Mediterranean Seafood* by Alan Davidson

YIELD
4 servings

PREPARATION
25 minutes

INGREDIENTS
12 ounces smoked whitefish (or sable or sturgeon)
1 apple
3 tomatoes
4 ounces Gouda cheese
2 cups sliced celery
1 small head Boston lettuce

DRESSING
1 cup plain yogurt
2 tablespoons oil
1 tablespoon lemon juice
½ teaspoon black pepper
½ teaspoon salt
Pinch of sugar (optional)
2 tablespoons chopped chives

Remove the skin ① and bones from the fish. Flake it off the bones ②.

Peel and dice the apple. Dice the tomatoes and cheese. Wash and trim the lettuce. Tear it into bite-size pieces and place in a salad bowl.

Add the celery, fish, fruit, and cheese to the salad bowl.

Mix the yogurt with the remaining dressing ingredients ③ and toss with salad. Chill for only a short time before serving.

YIELD
4 servings

PREPARATION
25 minutes

CHILLING
30 minutes

INGREDIENTS
4 ripe tomatoes
1 medium cucumber
½ package (10 ounces) frozen
   artichoke hearts
1 small fennel
1 large green bell pepper
1 medium onion
1 clove garlic
2 to 3 large red radishes
2 hard-cooked eggs
1 small can (2 ounces) anchovy fillets

1 can (6½ ounces) tuna, packed in oil
½ cup cooked lima beans
Lettuce leaves
Black olives
Chunks of french bread, toasted and
   spread with garlic butter

DRESSING
¼ cup red wine vinegar
¾ cup olive oil
Salt and freshly ground pepper

Quarter the tomatoes. Peel and slice the cucumber. Bring salted water to a boil and drop in the artichoke hearts; cook until tender, then drain and cool.

Slice the fennel into rings and cut rings in half. Core and seed the pepper, then slice into rings ①. Thinly slice the onion and mince the garlic. Slice the radishes and quarter or slice the eggs.

Drain the anchovy fillets and the tuna ②, then combine with the lima beans, tomatoes, cucumber, artichoke hearts, fennel, green pepper, onion, garlic, radishes, and eggs in a bowl ③.

Prepare the dressing by blending the vinegar with the oil and seasoning to taste with salt and pepper. Pour three-fourths of the dressing over the mixture and chill.

Line a salad bowl with lettuce leaves, then put in the nicoise mixture. Add the black olives and toss again, then drizzle on remaining dressing to preference. Top with the french bread and serve.

YIELD
4 to 6 servings

PREPARATION
20 minutes

CHILLING
2 hours

INGREDIENTS
1 cup dry white wine
1 tablespoon unflavored gelatin
1 cup water
1 tablespoon lemon juice
¼ cup sugar
½ cup sliced strawberries
½ cup sliced peaches
½ cup pitted cherries

Put ½ cup of the water into a small saucepan and add the gelatin. Soak for a few minutes, then set over low heat and stir until the gelatin dissolves. Stir in the lemon juice and sugar. Continue stirring until the sugar dissolves.

Remove the pan from the heat and add the remaining ½ cup of water and the wine. Chill the mixture until syrupy ①, then add the fruits ② and spoon the jelly into a 1-quart mold. Chill the mixture until thoroughly set. Unmold ③ and serve.

NOTE Recipe also works well when made with rosé wine; see photo.

From *The Salad Book* by Michele Evans

YIELD
4 servings

PREPARATION
25 minutes

INGREDIENTS
2 ripe papayas
1 firm banana
1 pint fresh strawberries
½ pint fresh raspberries
2 tablespoons chopped walnuts

DRESSING
2 tablespoons sugar
3 tablespoons water
1 tablespoon lemon juice
2 tablespoons dark rum

Halve the papayas and remove the seeds ①. Scoop out the pulp with a spoon and cut into strips ②. Reserve the shells.

Peel and slice the banana. Hull and halve the strawberries. Mix raspberries and walnuts with rest of salad.

Stir together the remaining ingredients and pour over fruit. Chill. When ready to serve, spoon the fruit into the reserved papaya shells ③.

A SALAD OF FRESH WILTED GREENS

YIELD
4 servings

PREPARATION
10 minutes

COOKING
20 minutes

INGREDIENTS
4 slices bacon
1/4 cup vinegar
1 head leaf lettuce, washed and cut
    into bite-size pieces
2 cups mixed greens (chicory,
    dandelion greens, romaine),
    washed and chopped
1/2 cup chopped scallions
Salt and pepper

Cut the bacon into small pieces, then sauté until crisp and drain on paper towels.

Add the vinegar to the bacon fat in the pan, then bring to a boil.

Put the greens in a salad bowl and add the scallions. Pour the vinegar mixture over and toss well. Season with salt and pepper, then garnish with the bacon bits.

SMOKED TURKEY SALAD

YIELD
4 servings

PREPARATION
10 minutes

INGREDIENTS
1 large onion, chopped fine
2 medium potatoes, cooked, peeled,
    and diced
1 cup cooked green beans
1 cup shredded smoked turkey breast
Chopped fresh parsley
Paprika

DRESSING
6 tablespoons oil
3 tablespoons vinegar or lemon juice
1/2 teaspoon salt
1 teaspoon dry mustard
Black pepper

In a bowl, mix together the onion, potatoes, beans, and turkey.

Add the dressing to moisten the mixture, then add more dressing if desired. Garnish with a sprinkling of fresh parsley or a dash of paprika.

DANISH CHEESE SALAD

YIELD
2 to 3 servings

PREPARATION
10 minutes

MARINATING
4 hours

INGREDIENTS

½ cup diced samsoe cheese (about 3½ ounces)
¼ cup crumbled Danish blue cheese (about 1 ounce)
1 sweet red pepper
1 green pepper
¼ cup corn oil
1 tablespoon fresh lemon juice
Dry mustard
Salt and freshly ground black pepper
1 sweet onion, finely chopped

Slice the peppers finely into rings, discarding the cores and seeds, and place the rings in a serving bowl.

Put the oil, lemon juice, a pinch of mustard, and salt and pepper to taste into a screw-top jar. Shake the mixture until well blended, then pour it over the peppers and let them marinate for 4 hours.

Add the cheeses and onion to the peppers and toss all of the ingredients together.

From *Everything Raw: The No-Cooking Cookbook* by Jennie Reekie

MELON CURRY SALAD

YIELD
3 or 4 servings

PREPARATION
15 minutes

INGREDIENTS

1 teaspoon curry powder
1 tablespoon fresh lemon juice
1 tablespoon cider vinegar
⅓ cup heavy cream
3 cups cubed cantaloupe or watermelon
Lettuce leaves

Mix the curry powder, lemon juice, and cider vinegar in a small bowl. Let the dressing stand for 5 minutes.

Whip the cream until thick but not really stiff. Stir the curry mixture gently into the whipped cream, then carefully mix in the melon cubes. Chill for 10 minutes.

Serve spooned into individual lettuce leaves.

From *The Best of Natural Eating Around the World* by Elizabeth Alston

INDEX